HOW THE HUMAN BODY WORKS

The Skeletal System

By Simon Rose

MEDIA ENHANCED BOOKS
AV²
BY WEIGL™
ADDED VALUE • AUDIO VISUAL

www.av2books.com

AV² provides enriched content that supplements and complements this book. Weigl's AV² books strive to create inspired learning and engage young minds in a total learning experience.

Your AV² Media Enhanced books come alive with...

Audio
Listen to sections of the book read aloud.

Key Words
Study vocabulary, and complete a matching word activity.

Video
Watch informative video clips.

Quizzes
Test your knowledge.

Go to www.av2books.com, and enter this book's unique code.

BOOK CODE

A832295

Embedded Weblinks
Gain additional information for research.

Slide Show
View images and captions, and prepare a presentation.

AV² by Weigl brings you media enhanced books that support active learning.

Try This!
Complete activities and hands-on experiments.

... and much, much more!

Published by AV² by Weigl
350 5th Avenue, 59th Floor
New York, NY 10118
Websites: www.av2books.com www.weigl.com

Library of Congress Cataloging-in-Publication Data
Rose, Simon, 1961- author.
Skeletal system / Simon Rose.
  pages cm. -- (How the human body works)
  Includes index.
ISBN 978-1-4896-1182-6 (hardcover : alk. paper) -- ISBN 978-1-4896-1183-3 (softcover : alk. paper) -- ISBN 978-1-4896-1184-0 (ebk.)
-- ISBN 978-1-4896-1185-7 (ebk.)
1. Skeleton--Juvenile literature. 2. Musculoskeletal system--Juvenile literature. I. Title.
QP301.R655 2015
612.7'51--dc23
                          2014005939

Printed in the United States of America in North Mankato, Minnesota
1 2 3 4 5 6 7 8 9 0 18 17 16 15 14

062014
WEP090514

Senior Editor Aaron Carr   Art Director Terry Paulhus

Photo Credits
Every reasonable effort has been made to trace ownership and to obtain permission to reprint copyright material. The publishers would be pleased to have any errors or omissions brought to their attention so that they may be corrected in subsequent printings.

Weigl acknowledges Getty Images as its primary image supplier for this title.

Contents

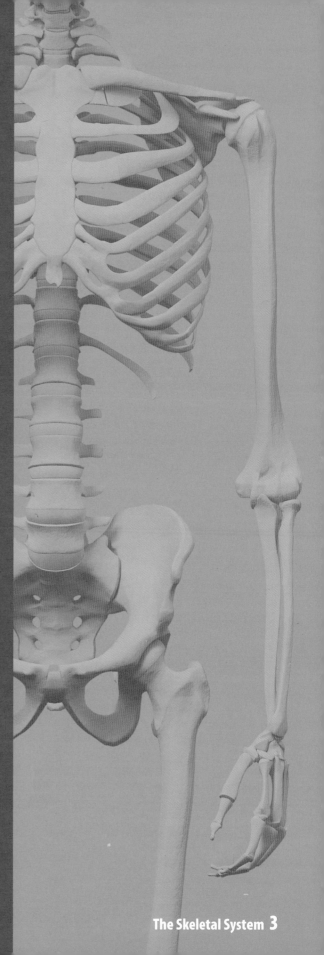

Human Body Systems

The human body is made up of complex systems. Each one plays an important role in how the body works. The systems are also interconnected. This means they work together.

For the body to stay healthy, its systems need to work together properly. Weakness or disease in one system can cause problems in one or more of the other systems. The most serious illnesses often affect several of the body's systems.

6 MAJOR BODY SYSTEMS

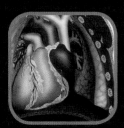

CARDIOVASCULAR SYSTEM

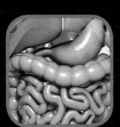

DIGESTIVE SYSTEM

MUSCULAR SYSTEM

NERVOUS SYSTEM

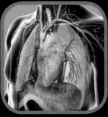

RESPIRATORY SYSTEM

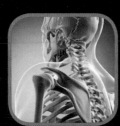

SKELETAL SYSTEM

SKELETAL SYSTEM

Acts as the blood factory of the body

Includes teeth, which are not made from bone

Calcium, iron, and energy in the form of fat are all stored in bones

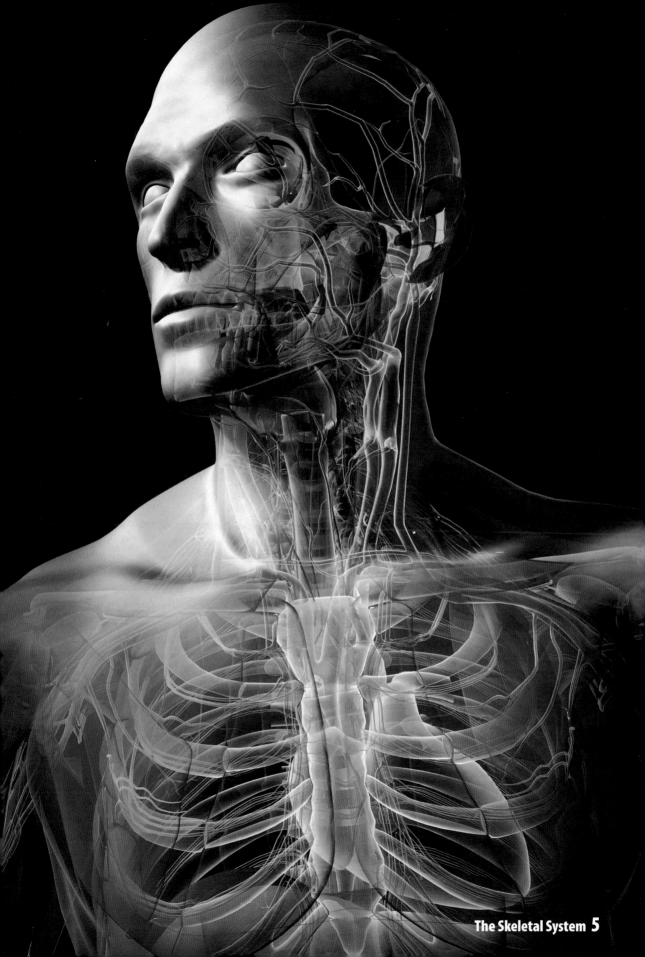

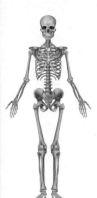

What Is the Skeletal System?

The skeletal system is a frame that supports the body and gives the body its shape. It includes bones as well as the **cartilage**, **ligaments**, and **tendons** that connect the bones to each other and hold the skeleton together. The skeletal system provides protection and support for the body's internal **organs**. The bones in the skull protect the brain, the bones of the spine protect the spinal cord, and the bones that make up the rib cage protect the heart and lungs.

People have about 300 bones when they are born. As people grow, many of these bones fuse together. By the age of 9 or 10, there are 206 bones in the skeletal system. These bones perform many important functions in the body. Bones are living organs. **Cells** inside human bones work to constantly break down old bone cells and create new cells to keep bones healthy and strong.

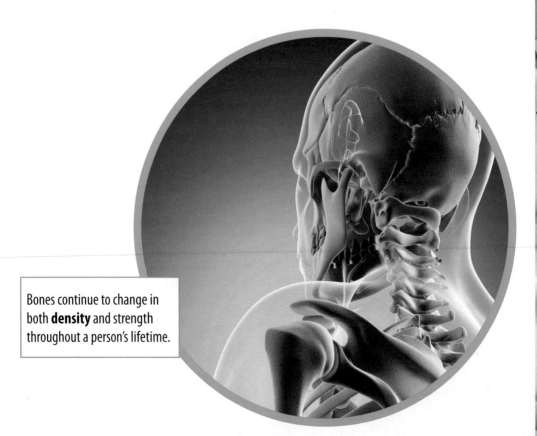

Bones continue to change in both **density** and strength throughout a person's lifetime.

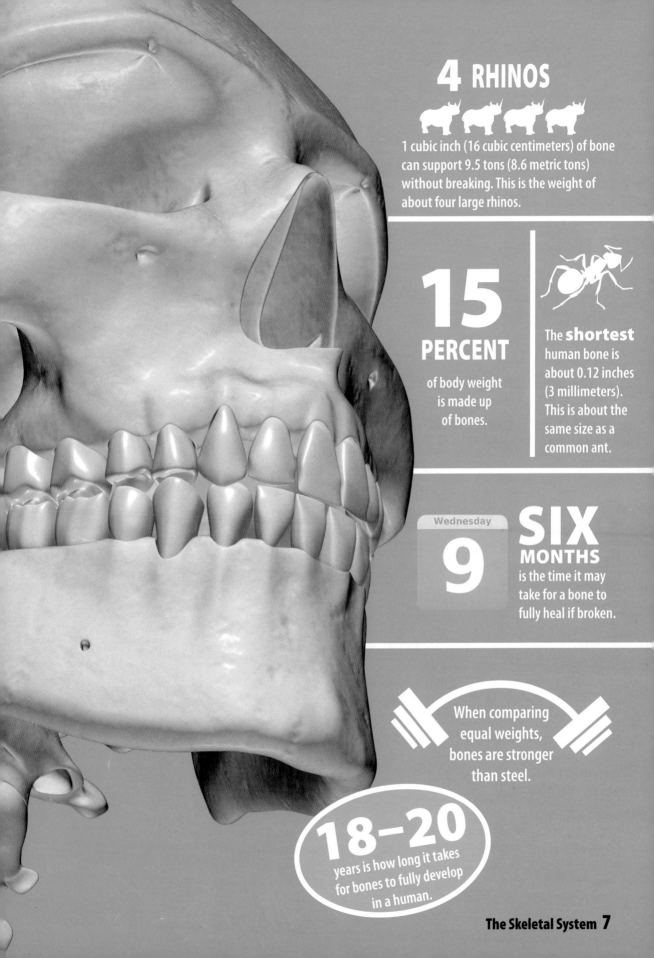

4 RHINOS

1 cubic inch (16 cubic centimeters) of bone can support 9.5 tons (8.6 metric tons) without breaking. This is the weight of about four large rhinos.

15 PERCENT

of body weight is made up of bones.

The **shortest** human bone is about 0.12 inches (3 millimeters). This is about the same size as a common ant.

Wednesday
9

SIX MONTHS

is the time it may take for a bone to fully heal if broken.

When comparing equal weights, bones are stronger than steel.

18–20

years is how long it takes for bones to fully develop in a human.

Skeletal System Features

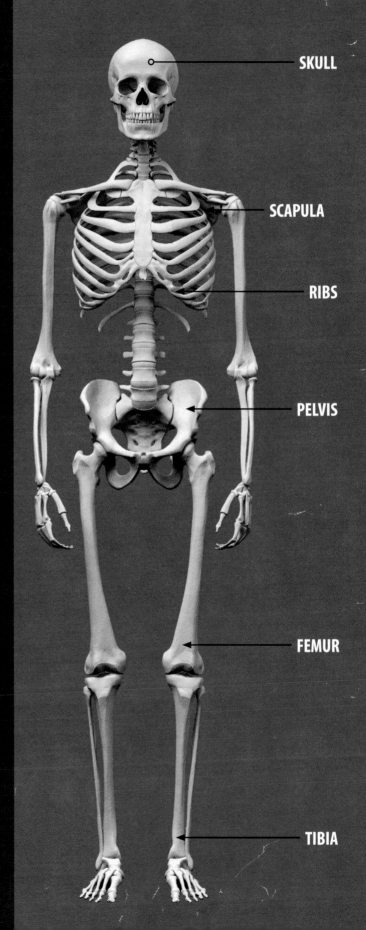

SKULL

SCAPULA

RIBS

PELVIS

FEMUR

TIBIA

The adult skeletal system has two main parts. The axial skeleton has 80 bones, including the skull, **hyoid**, ear bones, ribs, spine, and sternum, or breastbone. The appendicular skeleton contains 126 bones. These include the upper and lower limbs, the pelvis, and the scapula and other shoulder bones.

SKULL These bones are located at the top of the skeleton.

SCAPULA Also known as the shoulder blade, there is one on each side of the body.

RIBS The rib cage is formed by 12 pairs of ribs.

PELVIS This connects the upper bones to the lower limbs and has slight differences between males and females.

FEMUR This is the largest bone in the human body.

TIBIA This is the larger of the two bones that make up the lower leg.

Skull

The exact number of bones that make up the human skull varies depending on how the bones are counted. These bones include those found in the ear and the facial bones that support the eyes, mouth, and nose.

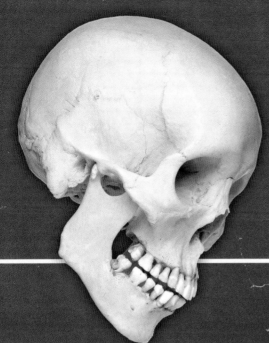

Foot

The lower leg bones known as the tibia and fibula connect to a large bone called the talus, or anklebone. The big toe has two small bones called phalanges, and the other toes each have three phalanges.

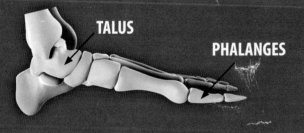

TALUS

PHALANGES

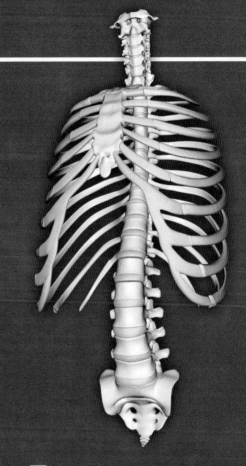

Hand

The bones of the lower arm connect with a group of eight smaller bones called the carpals to form the wrist joint. The palm of the hand is made up of five bones called metacarpals. The thumb has two bones called phalanges, while the fingers each have three.

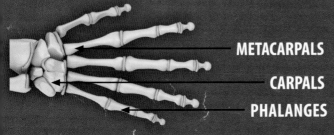

METACARPALS

CARPALS

PHALANGES

Torso

The torso is made up of bones that protect and support the heart, lungs, and major blood vessels of the body. The sternum is located in the middle of the chest. It is connected to the upper seven ribs by cartilage. The ribs are also connected to the spine.

How Does It Work?

People often think of a skeleton as a number of bones connected in the shape of a person. However, bones do not directly connect with one another. They are joined by connective tissues such as cartilage, tendons, and ligaments. Most skeletal muscles work by pulling bones either farther apart or closer together to create movement. The skeletal system's joints bend to allow the bones to move in many different directions.

Blood vessels inside bones provide the skeletal system with nutrients. The skeletal system stores nutrients and **minerals** that are essential to the health of the body. For example, bones store and release calcium into the blood supply when it is needed. Bone cells also release a **hormone** that helps regulate the body's blood sugar and fat deposits.

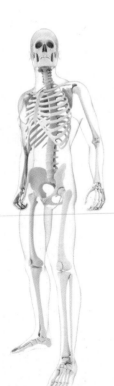

The Four Roles of the Skeletal System

PROTECT Bones protect vital organs from damage.

PRODUCE Bones are where the body's blood is made.

STORE Bones store and release minerals that are important to the body.

SUPPORT Bones support the other parts of the body.

Diagram of a Bone

A bone has a hard and dense outer layer, called compact bone. Beneath this is a layer of spongy bone, which is much lighter and more flexible. In the middle of some bones is a jelly-like substance called bone marrow.

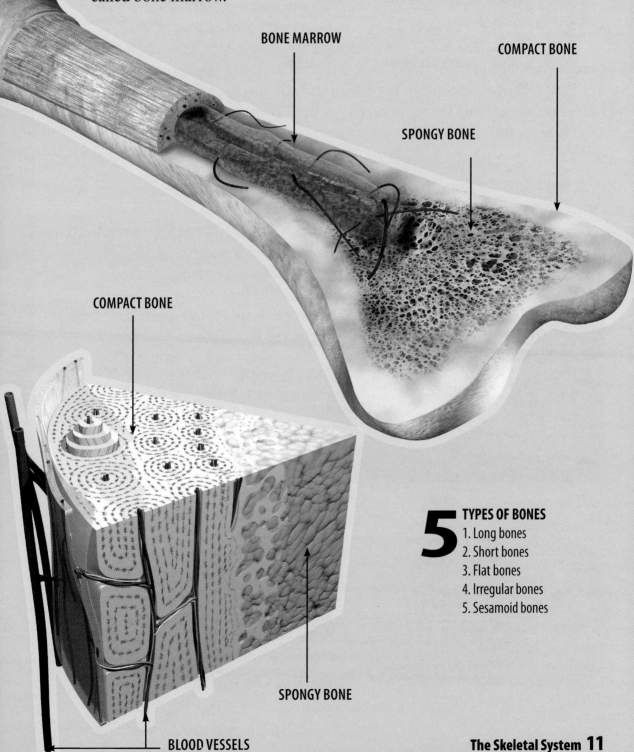

BONE MARROW

COMPACT BONE

SPONGY BONE

COMPACT BONE

SPONGY BONE

BLOOD VESSELS

5 **TYPES OF BONES**
1. Long bones
2. Short bones
3. Flat bones
4. Irregular bones
5. Sesamoid bones

The Skull

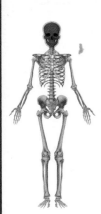

The skull is located in the top part of the axial skeleton. It is made up of 22 separate bones. The bones at the top of the skull form the cranium, which protects the brain. There are 14 facial bones that support the eyes, mouth, and nose. The bones are fused together by special joints, except for the mandible, or lower jaw. This is the only bone in the skull that is able to move. This allows people to chew food and talk. In children, the fused bones remain separate for the first years of life. This allows the brain and skull to grow and develop. The skull bones fuse together at about 2 years of age.

Anchors and Connectors

Other bones in the skull, such as the hyoid bone, anchor muscles in place.

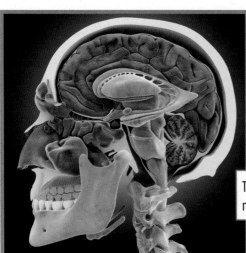

In the **middle ear**, three tiny bones connect the eardrum to the inner ear and help with hearing. These bones are the malleus, incus, and stapes. The stapes is the smallest bone in the human body.

The volume of an adult cranium is a little more than 1/3 of a gallon (1.3 liters).

The HUMAN SKULL by the Numbers

9 The weight of the average adult head is 9 pounds (4 kg).

32 A normal adult has 32 teeth, not counting wisdom teeth.

3 There are three bones in the ear that help people hear.

Diagram of a Skull

The bones of the skull do not only provide protection for vital organs, they also shape the outward appearance of each person.

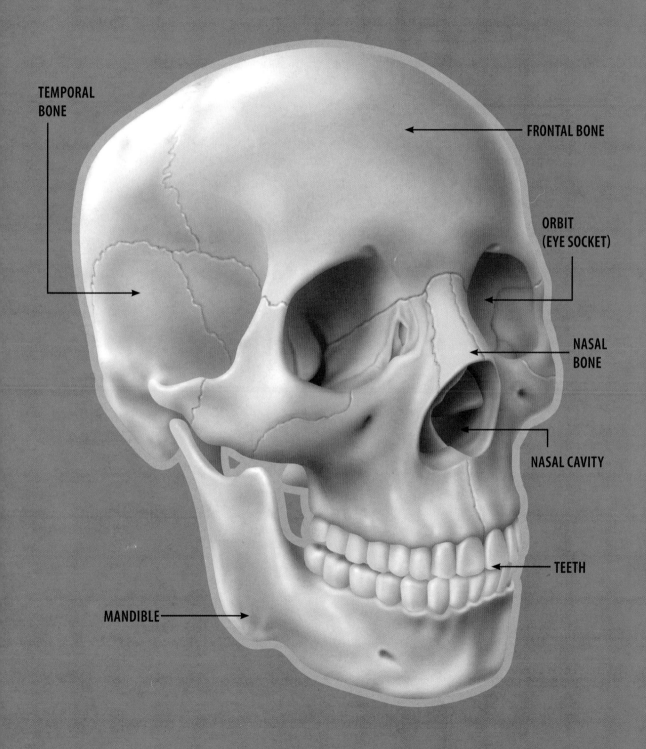

TEMPORAL BONE

FRONTAL BONE

ORBIT (EYE SOCKET)

NASAL BONE

NASAL CAVITY

TEETH

MANDIBLE

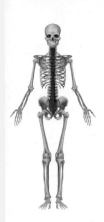

The Spine

The spine is made up of 24 **vertebrae** and two bones made of fused vertebrae. The vertebrae are attached to ligaments and muscles. Between each vertebra, disks made of cartilage serve as a kind of shock absorber to prevent damage to the bones.

Vertebrae

The seven vertebrae at the top of the spine support the head and neck. They are called cervical vertebrae. The first vertebra is called the atlas. It allows the head to move up and down. The second vertebra is called the axis. It allows the head and the atlas to move from side to side.

The 12 thoracic vertebrae are in the upper back. They connect to the ribs to form the rib cage. The five lumbar vertebrae are in the lower back. These bones are very strong because they carry the weight of the upper body. Below the lumbar vertebrae, the sacrum is a single bone made up of five vertebrae fused together. The coccyx, or tailbone, is at the base of the spine. It is a single bone fused from four vertebrae.

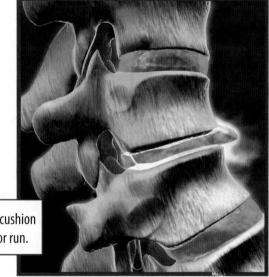

The disks between vertebrae cushion the spine when people walk or run.

The HUMAN SPINE by the Numbers

33
Before puberty, 33 bones make up the spine.

220
There are 220 ligaments in the spine.

Diagram of the Spine

With more than 100 joints and 120 muscles, the spine allows a wide range of motion. It also helps hold the body upright.

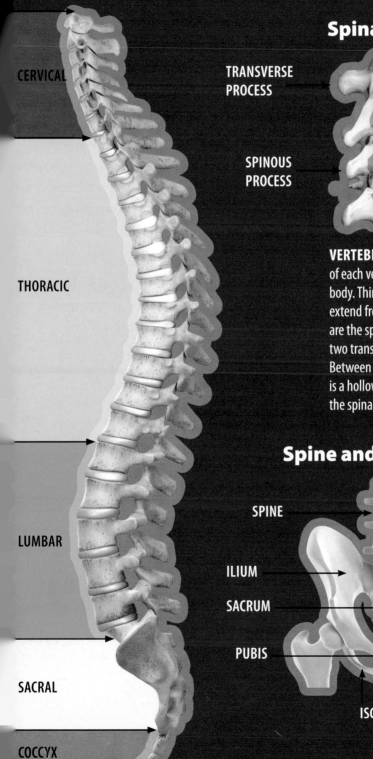

CERVICAL

THORACIC

LUMBAR

SACRAL

COCCYX

Spinal Column

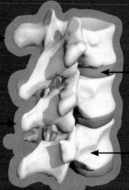

TRANSVERSE PROCESS

DISK

SPINOUS PROCESS

VERTEBRA

VERTEBRAE The main part of each vertebra is called the body. Thin columns of bone extend from the body. These are the spinous process and two transverse processes. Between these and the body is a hollow space that contains the spinal cord and **meninges**.

Spine and Pelvic Bones

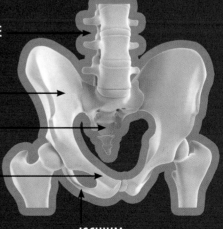

SPINE

ILIUM

SACRUM

PUBIS

ISCHIUM

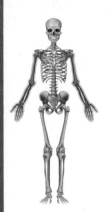

Arms and Hands

Each arm is attached to a scapula, or shoulder blade. This is a large, triangular bone on each side of the upper back. The upper arm contains the humerus. This bone connects to the scapula with a **ball and socket joint** at the shoulder. It also connects to the bones of the lower arm at the elbow.

The ulna and radius are the bones in the lower arm. They are wider at the ends to give them strength where they meet the joints. At the elbow, the ulna forms a joint with the humerus. The radius is the shorter of the two bones and is on the thumb side of the arm. It allows the hand and forearm to twist at the wrist. Both the ulna and the radius form a joint with the

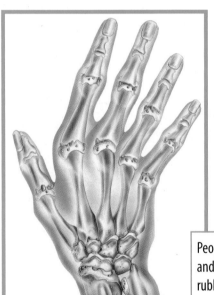

carpals. These eight small bones allow the wrist to move freely.

Staying Connected

All these bones are connected to tendons and muscles that support movement of the arms, hands, wrists, and shoulders.

People with osteoarthritis have limited movement and pain in their joints. This is caused by bones rubbing together at the joints.

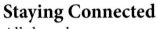

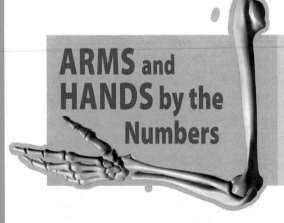

ARMS and HANDS by the Numbers

27

Each hand is made up of 27 bones.

19

There are 19 joints in each hand, with another eight in each wrist.

Diagram of Arms and Hands

The bones in the arms and hands are some of the most used and also the most vulnerable bones in the human body. Arms have some of the most commonly broken bones, making up almost half of all bone injuries in adults.

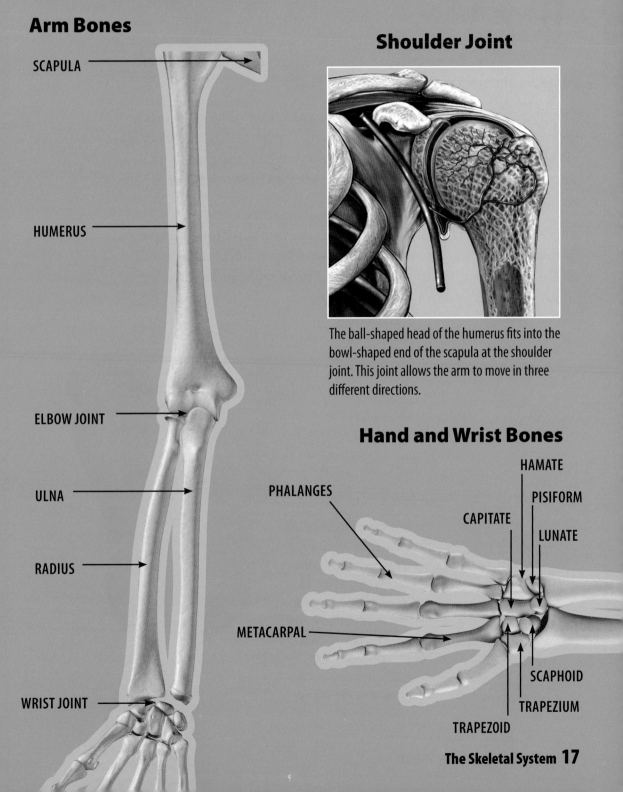

Arm Bones

SCAPULA

HUMERUS

ELBOW JOINT

ULNA

RADIUS

WRIST JOINT

Shoulder Joint

The ball-shaped head of the humerus fits into the bowl-shaped end of the scapula at the shoulder joint. This joint allows the arm to move in three different directions.

Hand and Wrist Bones

HAMATE

PISIFORM

CAPITATE

LUNATE

PHALANGES

METACARPAL

SCAPHOID

TRAPEZIUM

TRAPEZOID

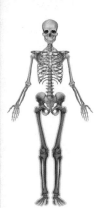

Legs and Feet

The left and right hipbones in the pelvic girdle connect the leg bones to the upper part of the skeleton. The femur, or thighbone, connects to the hipbone with a ball and socket joint. It also connects with the tibia and patella, or kneecap, to form the knee joint. The lower leg bones are the tibia and fibula.

The tibia, fibula, and the talus form the ankle joint. The talus is one of the seven tarsal bones located in the foot. The heel bone forms the base of the heel and is attached to the muscles that help the foot to move. The tarsals are seven small bones that make up the back part of the foot and heel.

There are joints between the tarsals and the foot's five long metatarsals. Each of these bones also forms a joint with the small phalanges of the toes. The bones in the foot are arranged to be wide and almost flat, allowing people to stand and walk.

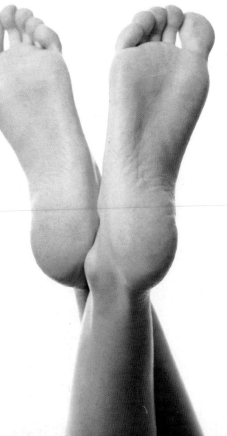

CARE FOR YOUR FEET

Human feet are not completely flat. The middle part of each foot is arched. Tendons in the feet pull the muscles into an arch. As people age, however, the tendons may become loose. This can result in a condition known as flat feet. To help prevent flat feet, people often wear shoes with arch support.

Leg and Foot Bones

The bones of the legs and feet help support the entire body. The two largest bones in the body, the femur and tibia, are both in the legs.

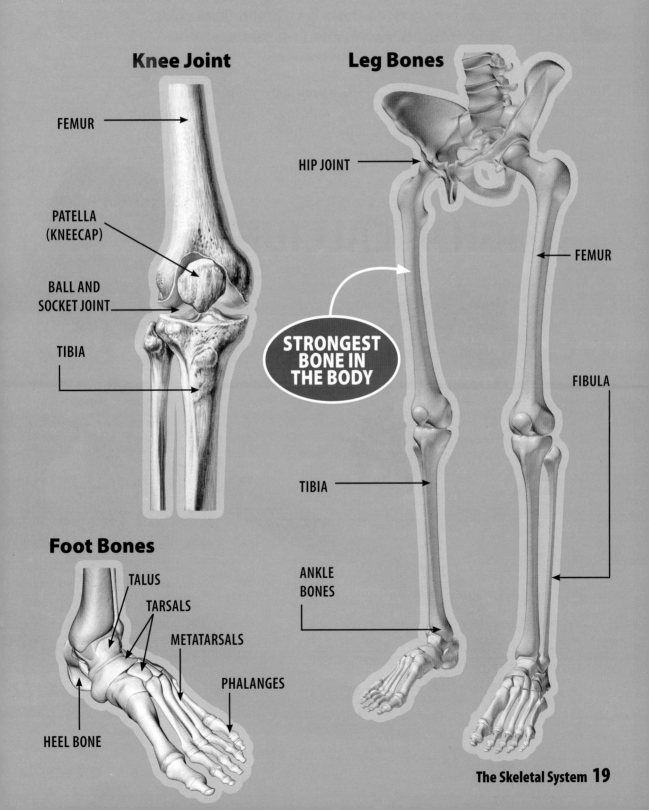

Knee Joint

FEMUR

PATELLA (KNEECAP)

BALL AND SOCKET JOINT

TIBIA

Leg Bones

HIP JOINT

FEMUR

STRONGEST BONE IN THE BODY

FIBULA

TIBIA

ANKLE BONES

Foot Bones

TALUS

TARSALS

METATARSALS

PHALANGES

HEEL BONE

Keeping Healthy

Staying healthy involves regular exercise and eating healthful foods. Calcium and vitamin D help maintain bone health. They can be found in a variety of foods, such as green vegetables.

Exercise

Some of the best ways to maintain healthy bones are weight-bearing exercises, such as jumping rope, running, walking, skiing, and climbing stairs. Maintaining a healthy body weight and lifting weights are other ways to keep bones strong.

HIGH IN CALCIUM

BROCCOLI

SPINACH

MILK

ALMONDS

Calcium-rich Foods

Milk is a source of calcium, but it is not the only one. Calcium is found in other dairy products, such as yogurt and cheese. Leafy green vegetables and fat-rich fish such as salmon also contain calcium. Some grain products, such as breakfast cereals, often have calcium added to them.

Vitamin D

The body needs vitamin D to help it absorb calcium. Vitamin D is found in beef liver, cheese, egg yolks, and in fish such as salmon, mackerel, and tuna. It is often added to milk and cereals as well.

Bone Disease

X-rays, bone density tests, and **MRIs** are used to detect diseases and problems in a person's skeletal system.

Osteoporosis is one of the most common bone diseases. It mostly affects older people. This disease causes bones to lose calcium, making them thinner and more likely to break.

Arthritis is a disease that damages the joints and areas around them in many parts of the body. Arthritis usually affects the joints of the hands, hips, knees, lower back, or shoulders.

25–30
YEARS OLD
This is the age at which bone density peaks for most people.

HIGH RISK
Up to 50% of women over the age of 50 in the U.S. are at risk for **osteoporosis.**

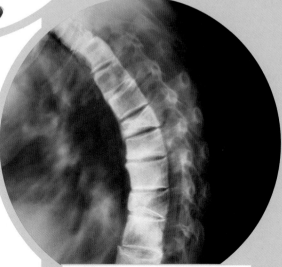

Scoliosis is a condition that creates a curve in the spine, which looks like a letter "S" or "C" when seen on an X-ray.

Studying the Skeletal System

Orthopedics is the field of medicine dedicated to the study and treatment of the skeletal system. Today, this is a specialized area of medicine, but people have been studying the human body and skeleton since ancient times.

1600 BC

Anatomy is studied in ancient Egypt. Accounts survive today in the Edwin Smith Surgical Papyrus, which dates from about 1600 BC. It is the oldest known record of medical practices.

FATHER OF MEDICINE

About 400 BC Considered to be the father of medicine in ancient Greece, Hippocrates wrote about treatment for dislocations of hips, knees, and shoulders, and for infections caused by broken bones piercing the skin.

1895

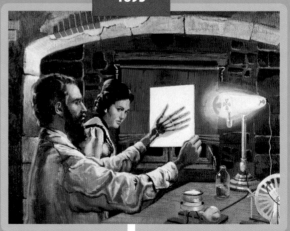

Wilhelm Conrad Röntgen discovers X-rays.

About 400 BC

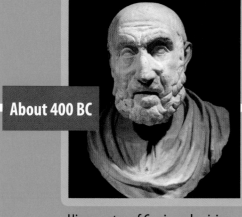

Hippocrates of Cos is a physician in ancient Greece. He is thought to be one of the most outstanding figures in the history of medicine.

About 300 BC

A school of anatomy is founded in the ancient Egyptian city of Alexandria.

Galen of Pergamon is a prominent Greek physician, surgeon, and philosopher. His work influences the practice of medicine throughout Europe until the mid-17th century.

AD 200

1832

The Anatomy Act in Great Britain makes it easier for doctors to obtain cadavers, or corpses used in medical research.

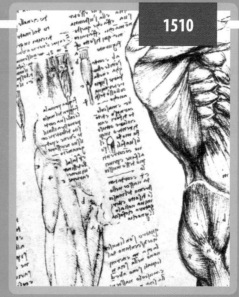

1510

Artist Leonardo da Vinci creates hundreds of drawings in a detailed study of human anatomy.

1973

Paul Lauterbur makes breakthroughs in developing the MRI. He later wins a Nobel Prize for his work.

2013

NASA awards $750,000 to scientists to study bone loss in space.

Working Together

No system in the human body works alone. All the systems must work together to keep people healthy and in **equilibrium**. The skeletal system works very closely with other important systems in the body.

Bones and Muscles

The skeletal system works with the muscular and nervous systems to allow the body to move. The ends of every skeletal muscle attach to a bone. The joints in places such as the knee, shoulder, elbow, hip, and neck also work with muscles so that the bones can move.

When people take part in physical activities, many body systems have to work harder to help the body work harder. This includes the skeletal and muscular systems moving the limbs, the cardiovascular system pumping more blood through the body, and the respiratory system bringing more air into the body.

ENERGY = MOTION

In order for the body to move, it must have energy. The body receives energy from food, which is processed by the digestive system.

Making Blood

The skeletal system works with the body's circulatory system to produce and transport blood. Bone marrow contained within the bones produces new blood cells. The circulatory system, which includes the heart and veins, then moves the blood throughout the body. Red blood cells transport oxygen to all parts of the body. White blood cells are part of the body's immune system, which helps protect the body from disease.

Athletes have to be careful not to overwork the body. They may suffer a sprain if they stretch a ligament too far.

650
muscles work with bones to move the body.

Protecting the Body

The bones of the skeletal system protect most of the other body systems. Bones protect the central nervous system from serious damage. The cranium protects the brain, and vertebrae protect the spinal cord. Bones also protect the vital organs of the respiratory system, such as the heart and lungs.

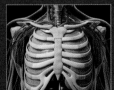

Careers

Some medical careers involve studying or working with the skeletal system. There are many exciting and challenging careers working with technology, research equipment, or treating injuries and disorders related to the skeletal system. Many jobs require a background in biology, physics, or computers. Before considering these careers, it is important to research options and learn about the education needed to work in a profession.

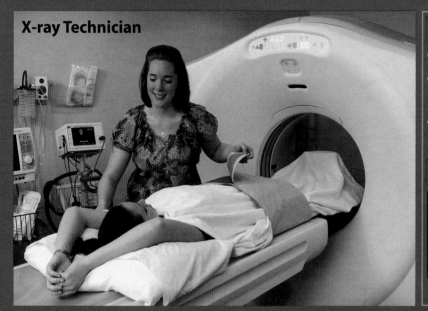
X-ray Technician

Education

- High school science and math
- Post-secondary associate's degree in radiography
- Must be licensed (varies by location)

Tools

X-ray Machine

X-ray Technician X-ray technicians use high-tech imaging machines to examine the inside of the body. The pictures they take help doctors to diagnose and treat diseases or injuries more effectively. Some X-ray technicians work with all kinds of patients, while others might specialize in medical conditions affecting specific parts of the body. X-ray technicians work in hospitals, doctor's offices, and specialized medical centers. Radiation is used in their work, so X-ray technicians follow strict safety rules and wear protective clothing when necessary.

Education

X-ray technicians take courses in anatomy, biology, and physics. They also learn about the effects of radiation and how to administer drugs to patients. Technicians need to take courses to upgrade their skills as technology changes.

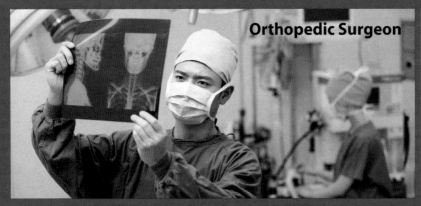

Orthopedic Surgeon

Years of Education
- Bachelor's degree: 4
- Medical school: 4
- Internship and residency: 5

Tools

Replacement Hip

Orthopedic Surgeon Orthopedic surgeons treat injuries to bones, joints, and muscles. They perform surgery, but they also use physical therapy or treatments, such as casts or splints, to heal injuries. Orthopedic surgeons work closely with other medical professionals to decide the best treatment for a patient.

Education

Orthopedic surgeons have to complete a bachelor's degree and four years of medical school. This is followed by five years of residency before they are ready to work as orthopedic surgeons.

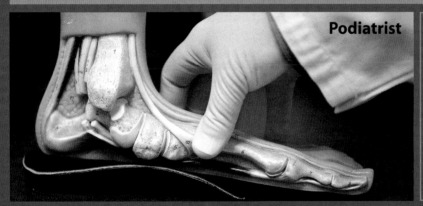

Podiatrist

Years of Education
- Bachelor's degree: 2–4
- Podiatry school: 4
- Residency: 1–2

Tools

Corrective Footwear

Podiatrist Podiatrists work with the bones and muscles of the feet, ankles, and legs. They diagnose and treat diseases, injuries, and other issues related to these parts of the body. Podiatrists use tools such as casts and corrective footwear to treat patients. Podiatrists play an important role in preventing foot, ankle, and leg injuries in athletes.

Education

To attend a school of podiatric medicine, students must complete at least two years of a bachelor's degree. However, most students finish the bachelor's degree before applying. Podiatry school is an additional four years. Some schools also require a one- or two-year residency at a hospital or clinic.

The Skeletal System Quiz

T est your knowledge of the skeletal system by answering these questions. The answers are provided below for easy reference.

1 What is the largest bone in the human body?

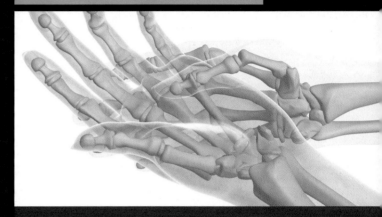

4 How many bones make up each hand?

7 What is the shortest bone in the human body?

10 What bone disease damages the joints and the areas around them?

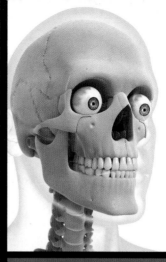

2 What are the small bones in the fingers called?

3 How many bones are in the skull?

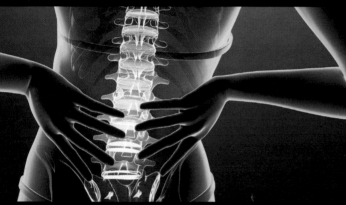

6 What is another name for the scapula?

5 What acts as a kind of natural shock absorber between each vertebra?

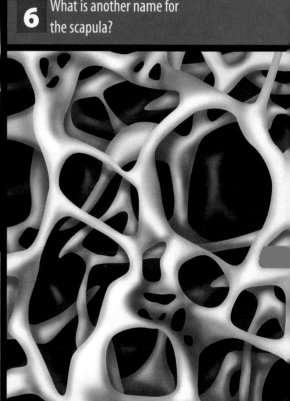

8 What is produced by bone marrow?

9 What vitamin is important for maintaining healthy bones?

Activity

Complete this activity to see how important calcium is in maintaining bone structure and strength.

Losing Calcium

BEFORE YOU START, YOU WILL NEED:

2 clean, dried chicken or turkey leg bones

1 large container or jar with a lid

2 to 3 cups (0.5 to 0.7 L) of vinegar

1 Make sure your chicken bones are clean and dry. Try to bend them. Are they difficult to bend?

2 Place one bone in the jar, and fill the jar with enough vinegar to cover the bone completely.

3 Put the lid on the jar so it is completely sealed.

4 Put the jar in a safe place where the temperature will not change, and leave your chicken bone to soak in the vinegar for about 4 days.

5 Leave the other bone beside the jar, exposed to open air.

6 Check on the bone in the jar periodically. The calcium carbonate in the bone should be reacting with the mild acid of the vinegar. Look for small bubbles forming inside the jar.

7 On the fourth day, open the jar. Remove the bone from the jar, and dispose of the vinegar.

8 Try to bend the bone now. Has anything changed? How does it compare to the bone that was outside the jar? Why do you think this may be?

Key Words

ball and socket joint: a joint in which the ball-shaped end of a bone fits into a cup-shaped indent of another bone

cartilage: connective tissue found in various parts of the body, such as the joints

cells: the smallest structures of the human body from which all organs and systems are made

density: a measure of how much material is packed into a given space

equilibrium: a state of total balance

hormones: substances produced in various organs that help regulate the body

hyoid: a U-shaped bone in the neck; supports the tongue

ligaments: tissues that connect to bones or cartilage at a joint or supports an organ

meninges: membranes covering the brain and spinal cord

middle ear: the main opening of the ear; separated from the external ear opening by the eardrum

minerals: natural materials the body needs to stay healthy

MRIs: magnetic resonance imaging machines used to produce images of the soft tissues of the body

organs: self-contained parts of the body that serve a particular function; two or more organs working together create a body system

tendons: tissues that connect muscle to nearby bones

vertebrae: the bones of the spinal column

X-rays: radiation used to examine the bones inside the body

Index

Log on to www.av2books.com

AV² by Weigl brings you media enhanced books that support active learning. Go to www.av2books.com, and enter the special code found on page 2 of this book. You will gain access to enriched and enhanced content that supplements and complements this book. Content includes video, audio, weblinks, quizzes, a slide show, and activities.

AV² Online Navigation

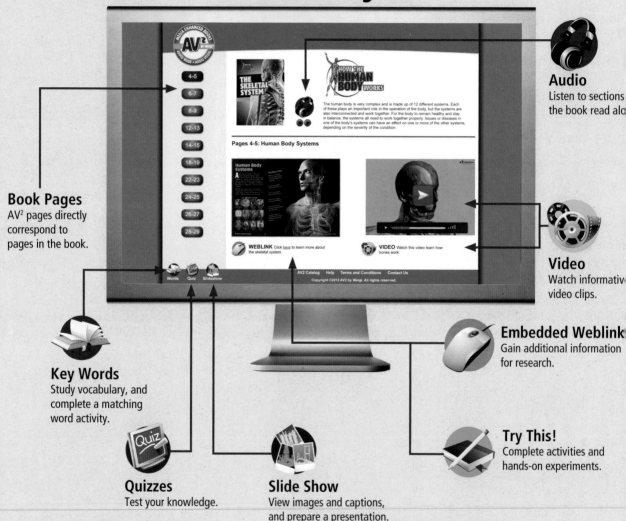

Book Pages
AV² pages directly correspond to pages in the book.

Audio
Listen to sections the book read alo...

Video
Watch informativ... video clips.

Key Words
Study vocabulary, and complete a matching word activity.

Embedded Weblink
Gain additional information for research.

Try This!
Complete activities and hands-on experiments.

Quizzes
Test your knowledge.

Slide Show
View images and captions, and prepare a presentation.

AV² was built to bridge the gap between print and digital. We encourage you to tell us what you like and what you want to see in the future.

Sign up to be an AV² Ambassador at www.av2books.com/ambassador.